American Jukebox

American Jukebox

★ The Classic Years ★

VINCENT LYNCH

PHOTOGRAPHY by KAZ TSURUTA

CHRONICLE BOOKS • SAN FRANCISCO

Jukebox advertisements courtesy of The Wurlitzer Company.

Printed in Japan.

Library of Congress Cataloging in Publication Data

    Lynch, Vincent.
       American jukebox, the classic years / Vincent Lynch.
          p.   cm.
       ISBN 0-87701-722-0. — ISBN 0-87701-678-X (pbk.)
       1. Jukeboxes—Pictorial works.   I. Title.
    ML 1081.L88 1990
    621.389′33—dc20   90−1687
                                     CIP
                                     MN

Book and cover design: Julie Noyes
Cover photograph: Kaz Tsuruta

Distributed in Canada by Raincoast Books,
112 East Third Avenue, Vancouver, B.C. V5T 1C8

10 9 8 7 6 5 4 3 2 1

Chronicle Books
275 Fifth Street
San Francisco, CA 94103

This book is dedicated to the loving memory of my father,
Thomas Edward Lynch, one of the original "snappy steppers."

CONTENTS

TURN IN YOUR OLD INSTRUMENTS

WITH ASSURANCE THAT THEY WILL NEVER AGAIN COMPETE WITH YOU FOR ANY LOCATION

SMASHED TO PIECES

WURLITZER REALLY SMASHES THEM!

• Every obsolete phonograph turned in under Wurlitzer's Factory Trade-In Plan on Wurlitzer Model 500 or 600 Phonographs goes direct to the nearest of 28 bonded warehouses where it is quickly and totally demolished. Nothing is saved. There is no chance that these old instruments will ever appear again on any location.

Only Wurlitzer guarantees total destruction of all phonographs traded in—takes this progressive step as part of its program to stabilize Music Merchant operations and enable Wurlitzer Music Merchants everywhere to make more money.

INTRODUCTION

The American Jukebox: 1937–1948

In the 1930s and 1940s, the jukebox craze swept America. Jukeboxes found a place in restaurants, taverns, malt shops, school auditoriums, honky-tonks, USOs and wartime canteens, and had tremendous impact on popular culture and in molding America's taste in music.

Without two of Thomas A. Edison's 1,093 U.S. patents, the light bulb and the phonograph, the jukebox would not exist. Edison announced the invention of the phonograph in 1877. His machine impressed sound wave modulations onto a sheet of tinfoil, reproduced the sound acoustically, and played through a listening tube without amplification and without the use of electricity.

Though Edison intended this as a business device, its application to reproduce music was swift. One of his machines was fitted with a coin slot and installed by Louis Glass on November 23, 1889, at the Palais Royal Saloon in San Francisco. It was the first known coin-operated phonograph, and within a week was earning $15 per day. Four listening tubes enabled a quartet of listeners to hear a few minutes of music for a nickel each. In a short time Mr. Glass installed coin mechanisms on twelve other Edison machines and placed them in other establishments; the novelty proved profitable, and through the 1890s variations of the coin-operated player made music from wax and cardboard cylinders in phonograph parlors in cities across the country and in Europe.

In 1906 the John Gabel Company introduced the Automatic Entertainer, the first coin-operated phonograph to offer more than one selection, and one of the first to use discs instead of cylinders. "Power" was supplied by a hand crank; after the spring mechanism was wound, the machine operations functioned automatically. The Entertainer featured a 40-inch horn for sound amplifica-

tion, a slug rejector and a visible phonograph mechanism—innovations that heralded the modern jukebox.

The advent of radio created demand for popular music, and in the same period, the phonograph was becoming a more common fixture in affluent homes. The first electric phonograph, the Brunswick Panatrope, was introduced in 1924. It had an A/C power supply, an electronic motor turntable, a vacuum tube amplifier and the first dynamic speaker to be used on home equipment. The electric speaker's ability to deliver extremely loud volume with thundering bass found immediate public acceptance. This was no longer a parlor curiosity for a small group of friends: with electric amplification, large groups could be entertained.

In 1927, the Automated Musical Instruments Company (AMI) introduced a 20-selection, coin-operated, electrically amplified phonograph that played both sides of ten electronically recorded 78 rpm discs. The J. P. Seeburg Company hastily released the Melatone the same year. It was a disaster. The mechanism destroyed records and all 100 machines had to be recalled. Undaunted, Seeburg retooled and successfully released the Audiophone in 1928, an 8-selection model encased in a nickelodeon cabinet.

In 1928, Homer E. Capehart released the Orchestrope; it played 56 selections sequentially with no selectability. Capehart later went on to become Wurlitzer's marketing wizard, and a U.S. senator. He also operated the Packard Manufacturing Co. at various times in the thirties and forties, producing the well-engineered Packard Manhattan and Pla-Mor jukeboxes.

The Mills Novelty Co., which got its start with arcade machines and gambling devices, released the 12-selection Dance Master in 1929. The two other giants of the thirties and forties, Wurlitzer and Rock-Ola, didn't enter the field until 1933 and 1935, respectively, after the repeal of Prohibition. Wurlitzer, founded in the 1800s by German immigrant Rudolph Wurlitzer, was already renowned for its player pianos, carousel organs and ``mighty'' movie palace pipe organs. Despite the myth, the name Rock-Ola had nothing to do with rock 'n' roll. Rock-Ola was founded by Canadian-born manufacturer David C. Rockola, who got his start with penny scales.

Seeburg and AMI rode a tidal wave of tremendous demand until the stock market crash of 1929. Seeburg went into receivership in 1931, and not until the repeal of Prohibition did sales increase. By late 1933, Seeburg paid off their debts and resumed full production.

Between 1933 and 1938 the designs of the four major manufacturers featured visible mechanisms and wood cabinets that resembled a blend of a nickelodeon and an enlarged radio console with neoclassical motifs. In 1938, the drab-furniture approach to design was al-

tered forever with the introduction of translucent plastic. With the innovation of illuminated plastic, the modern jukebox was born!

The word "jukebox" entered our language in the late 1930s. Of the several etymological explanations, the most plausible seems that it came from the southern part of the United States. Blacks in the South used the

word "juke," meaning to dance. This slang word had its roots in Afro-American slang of the South. The "jook box" became the jukebox, a name that has stuck to this day.

The jukebox was the only venue for many artists other than live performances. In an effort to establish its respectability, early radio was elitist and played only classical or mainstream pop hits. Often, major white pop artists would "cover" hits made famous by black artists. The jukebox was the only way many fans of rhythm and blues, gospel, hillbilly and cowboy music could hear their favorite stars, especially if they couldn't afford a radio, much less a phonograph and records.

The jukeboxes in this book are from the Golden Age of the jukebox, 1937 to 1948. It was the Golden Age not only in terms of design, but also in terms of its importance to American culture. In every American community it was an intrinsic part of local gathering spots, from the malt shop to the tavern. The jukebox was the primary entertainment device in these establishments during the pre-television era. Unlike radio, favorite songs could be selected and played over and over again.

By 1939, an estimated 225,000 jukeboxes were playing. At a time when sales of home phonographs were waning, jukeboxes had a tremendous, positive impact on record companies: jukeboxes consumed 13 million discs a year. Prior to the outbreak of World War II, sales of records rocketed to 127 million, of which jukebox sales accounted for more than 50 percent.

From 1938 to 1940, the jukebox industry's production exploded. Major manufacturers released full-sized light-up jukeboxes, countertop models, wall boxes, bar boxes and speakers. In 1938, AMI introduced the first wall box, the Mighty Midget. The other companies quickly followed.

The Seeburg Play-boy, released in 1939, was a "wireless" wall box with a speaker below. The "wireless" units were plugged into ordinary A/C outlets. Electronic impulses were sent to the jukebox on the house's wiring, making selections and returning them to the unit's speaker the same way. This "stroller" type wall box could be rolled around to individual tables for convenience in making selections.

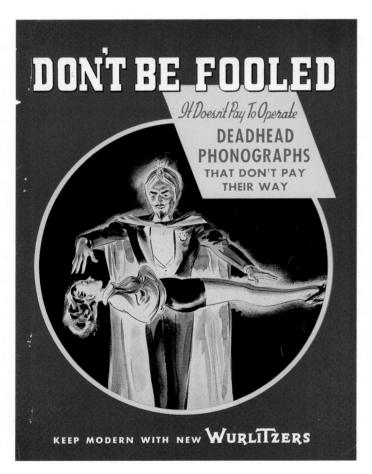

As a result of the profound impact of the introduction of plastics on the industry, ancillary companies sprang up, manufacturing kits to modernize old jukeboxes or to put old mechanisms into new light-up "universal" cabinets. The old-furniture look vanished.

The pioneers who led the plastic revolution were Nils Miller of Seeburg and Paul Fuller of Wurlitzer. Noel Marshall Seeburg, son of the Swedish-born founder, brought Miller into the company and he immediately began to experiment with phenolic resins. In 1938 his results were revealed with Seeburg's introduction of the Concert Grand, Regal and Gem models. If the credit for perfection of this innovation goes to Miller, Paul Fuller wins recognition for his manipulation of the medium in the most original and unique way, turning a utilitarian device into an art object.

To fend off corporate espionage, Fuller developed his concepts in a special high-security enclosure at Wurlitzer. When the enigmatic Fuller finished each design, he reportedly would come out of the design studio and say, "Here it is!"—and the factory would produce it. Wurlitzer enabled him to become the undisputed master of jukebox design. In his tenure there, Fuller created thirteen full-sized boxes, five countertop models, one freestanding small console, seventeen extension speakers and all the wall boxes Wurlitzer produced between 1938 and 1948. The 1941 Model 850 was one of his greatest innovations. It used revolving discs of polarized film and varying thicknesses of colorless cellophane to create prisms of moving, changing colors to dazzle and enchant onlookers. As an artist, he appreciated the freedom to create without compromise or interference. Wurlitzer's confidence paid off in extraordinary sales, making it the preeminent company of the era.

Manufacturers continued to experiment with new ways to deliver music to patrons. In 1939, AMI introduced the

Automatic Hostess telephone system and in 1941 Rock-Ola invented the Mystic Music System. Both were jukeboxes in every way except there was no phonograph mechanism. After depositing a coin, the patron spoke into a microphone to an operator who would play the selection; the music returned over the phone lines to the speaker. The systems proved unsuccessful for AMI and Rock-Ola, but the idea worked for the Shyver Multiphone Co., which operated in Seattle, Tacoma and Olympia, Washington, from 1939 to 1959.

The industry boomed in the early 1940s until Pearl Harbor. On December 11, 1941, the government directed jukebox and other coin-operated machine manufacturers to immediately cut production by 75 percent.

Jukeboxes were considered nonessential products in the war effort. The major manufacturers issued "Victory Models," such as the Wurlitzer 950, the Seeburg Minute Man Hi-tone 9200, the Rock-Ola Commando and the AMI 40-selection Singing Tower, before production ceased in the spring of 1942. The companies retooled and joined the rest of American industry to focus on the war effort.

Working under government contracts with frantic production deadlines, the jukebox factories went on three eight-hour shifts per day to manufacture essential products for the war. Wurlitzer made electronic devices for tanks and the signal corps, de-icing equipment and other aircraft components. Rock-Ola went from music to munitions, producing rifles and ammunition boxes. Seeburg specialized in electromechanics, making the "Intervalometer," a device that time-released bombs. Seeburg's wartime research would not be appreciated by the musical public until the late forties and early fifties with the introduction of the revolutionary Model M100-A.

The wartime economy was booming with increased employment. People longed for diversion; fanned by scarcity, the demand for jukeboxes ignited. Operators sold old jukeboxes for triple the pre-war price. "Universal" light-up cabinets were made by independents to

Wurlitzer Music Merchants

I APPRECIATE THE IMPORTANT PART YOU PLAY IN THE DAILY LIVES OF THE AMERICAN PEOPLE HELP ME SELL NATIONAL DEFENSE BONDS

SHOW YOUR PATRIOTISM. PLACE A RECORDING OF "Any Bonds Today?" IN No. 1 POSITION ON EVERY PHONOGRAPH OR WALL BOX YOU OPERATE

DON'T FAIL ME AND I WON'T FAIL YOU

Uncle Sam

LET'S HELP HIM PUT IT ACROSS

house old recycled mechanisms. Wurlitzer produced 18,000 of the famous Victory cabinet between 1943 and 1945, designed to house the components of older models, using glass instead of plastic in the side panels.

Jukeboxes were also an extremely important morale booster at USOs and oversea bases of the Armed Forces. It was a way "our boys" kept a musical umbilical cord to the heartland to escape for a few moments the horrors of war.

In 1945, at the end of the war, manufacturing restrictions were rescinded and a new race was on. Seeburg released the first new model, the S-146. It wasn't popular with operators because the mechanism wasn't visible and held less fascination for patrons. Nicknamed the "Trash Can" because of its hinged red dome lid and barrel shape, it initially sold well because there was nothing else on the market. Rock-Ola launched the Magic-Glo series with Models 1422, 1426 and 1428 between 1946 and 1948. In 1946, AMI presented one of the largest and most garish jukeboxes ever designed, the 40-selection Model A, or, as it was affectionately called, the "Mother of Plastic." AMI offered the greatest choice of musical selections; the other companies only offered 20- to 24-selection boxes. Selectability alone, however, was not enough to challenge the ultimate jukebox of all time, the Wurlitzer Model 1015, released in 1946.

Wurlitzer embarked on the most extensive publicity campaign in jukebox history for the bubble-tubed, color-changing 1015. In a departure from the past, when manufacturers had focused on convincing operators to buy their products, Wurlitzer went to the public to increase brand recognition. The Wurlitzer logo appeared on billboards, swizzle sticks, napkins, decals, illuminated signs and tabletops. A massive print and

billboard campaign featured folksy scenes of people enjoying the American way of life with the Model 1015. The message was clearly stated in their post-war billboards: "Wurlitzer is Music!" Nearly 60,000 units of the Model 1015 were manufactured, the most of any jukebox ever made.

By the end of 1947, Wurlitzer had shipped 80,000 jukeboxes, over 70 percent of the output of the entire in-

2 MOVE PHONOGRAPHS FORMERLY IN BEST LOCATIONS TO SECOND BEST PLACES

• As second step in modernization program, music merchants replace instruments in second best locations with more modern, higher earning phonographs formerly in their best locations. Immediate increase in earnings from second best locations results under stimulus of improved cabinet illumination, superior tone and 24 record carrying capacity enabling location to meet the varied music tastes of all patrons.

3 MOVE PHONOGRAPHS FORMERLY IN SECOND BEST LOCATIONS TO THIRD BEST PLACES

• As third step in modernization program, music merchants move phonographs formerly in second best spots to third best locations. Results? Greater earnings from these places, too, as profits from entire operation go up under application of step by step modernization program made possible by Wurlitzer's Factory Trade-In Plan. Old instruments originally in these locations are traded in to be totally destroyed.

ONLY WURLITZER'S TRADE-IN PLAN GUARANTEES COMPLETE DESTRUCTION OF OBSOLETE INSTRUMENTS

dustry. The 1948 Model 1100 was the last Wurlitzer of the Golden Age and was a bit of a disappointment to the company. As the country moved into a mild recession, the bottom fell out of the jukebox market and Wurlitzer overestimated production, ending up with a large overstock of machines. Only 16,200 Model 1100s were produced. It was the end of an era of dominance that had lasted over ten years.

In an effort to cash in on the tremendous demand in the post-war period, smaller companies sprang up, such as Aireon, Pantages, Filben, H. C. Evans, and Homer E. Capehart's Packard. In December 1948, Seeburg introduced the Model M100-A, a 100-selection jukebox. It was so revolutionary that it took at least three years for other manufacturers to catch up. It set the tone for jukebox styling and electronics for the next twelve years, and secured for Seeburg the industry dominance in the fifties that Wurlitzer had enjoyed in the forties.

Despite the Great Depression and World War II, the jukebox triumphed. The government may have declared jukeboxes a nonessential product of "The War Machine," but the public's desire for them proved them an essential product for "The Human Machine." They brought the gift of music to elevate the human spirit. Listening to these jukeboxes was an emotional, sensual event. Eyes were dazzled by the light display as ears were entertained by a favorite band playing a command performance for just one nickel.

I've seen pairs of initials carved into the sides of old, unrestored boxes. Although this undoubtedly irked operators at the time, it is symbolic to me of America's romance with the jukebox. Because of the dedication of collectors to preserve the past, we are able, in this book, to experience these extraordinary machines from the jukebox's Golden Age, 1937 to 1948. The attention to detail in restoration reveals them as they were seen in their prime. As you peruse these pages, "listen" to the photographs; see with your eyes and hear with your heart. America's love affair was based as much on the jukebox as an object as on the music it played. America may have invented the jukebox, but she doesn't own it. The jukebox belongs to the world!

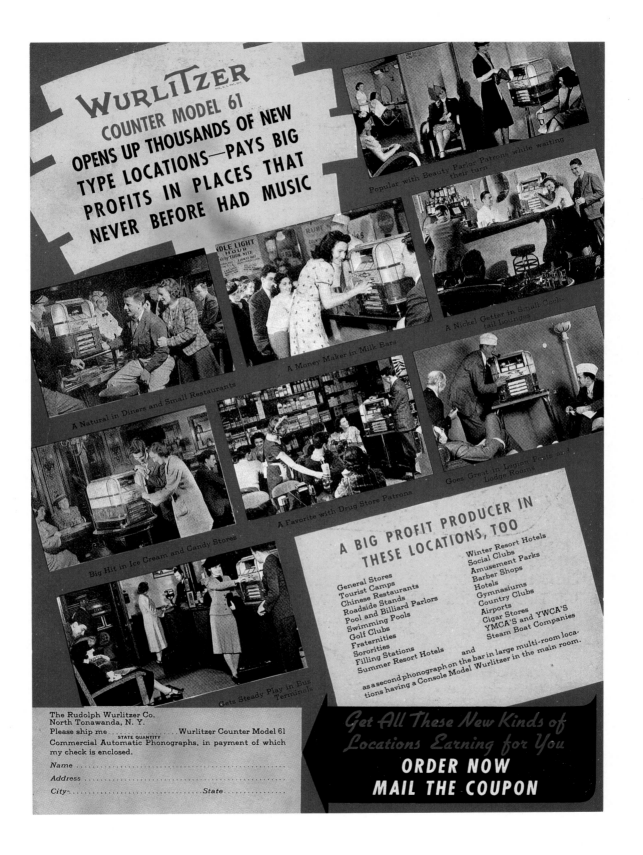

FULL-SIZED JUKEBOXES

THE SATURDAY EVENING POST

Good Tip for a Good Time —
WURLITZER MUSIC

Look for the Sign of the Musical Note

In the mood for music? Want to have fun? Here's a tip that guarantees a good time. Stop where you see the Wurlitzer Sign of the Musical Note. It's a gay little sign that says, "Here you'll have fun because we have Wurlitzer Music."

It's music by the best bands in the land that works magic in stimulating gaiety...in stirring up fun...in assuring a grand time for everyone.

Take your pick of 24 tunes. New hits, old favorites, novelty numbers—they're all there for your pleasure. As you listen you'll learn why folks of all ages vote Wurlitzer Phonograph Music America's favorite musical pastime. The Rudolph Wurlitzer Company, North Tonawanda, New York.

The *Sign of the Musical Note* identifies places where you can have fun playing a Wurlitzer.

THE NAME THAT MEANS *Music* **TO MILLIONS**

The music of Wurlitzer pianos, accordions, electronic organs, and juke boxes is heard "'round the world." Wurlitzer is America's largest manufacturer of pianos all produced under one name... also America's largest, best known manufacturer of juke boxes and accordions.

Wurlitzer Model 24, 1938

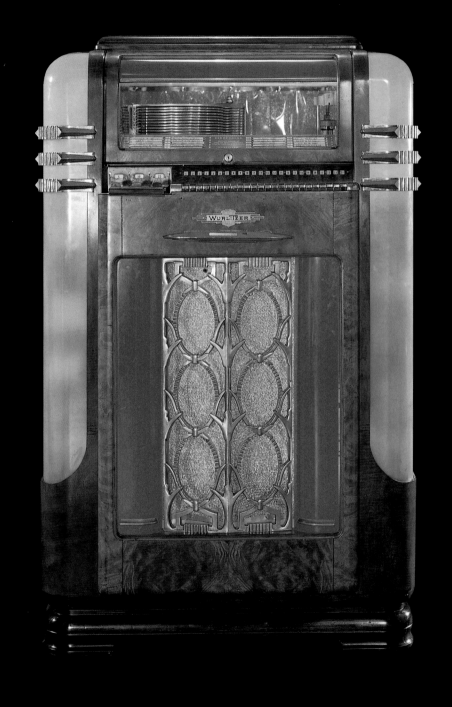

Mills Empress, 1939

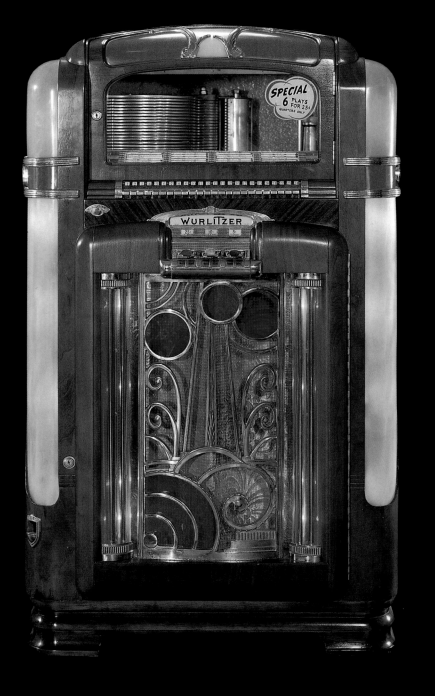

Seeburg Envoy, 1940

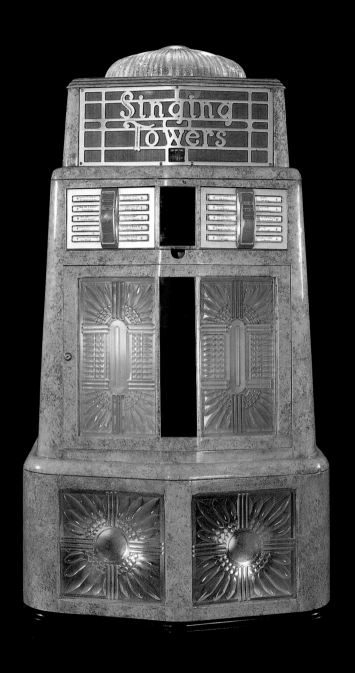

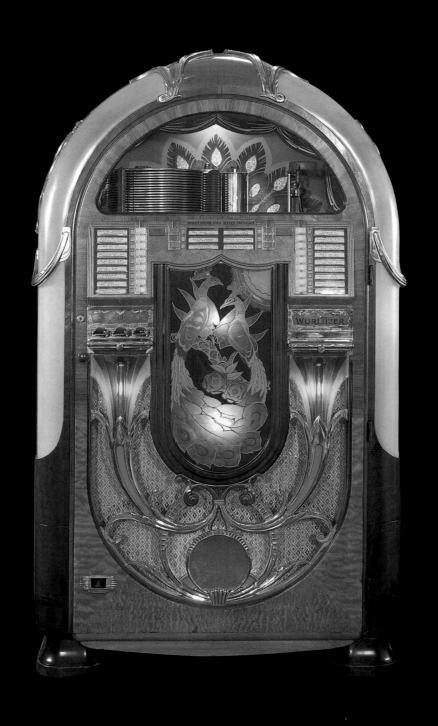

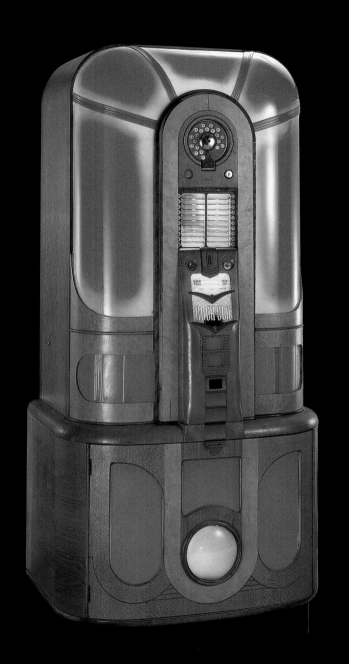

Rock-Ola Model 1422, 1946

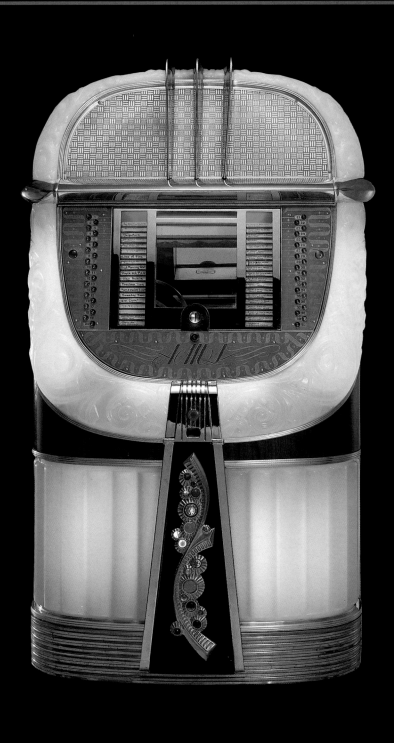

AMI Model A, Mother of Plastic, 1946

Filben Maestro, 1946

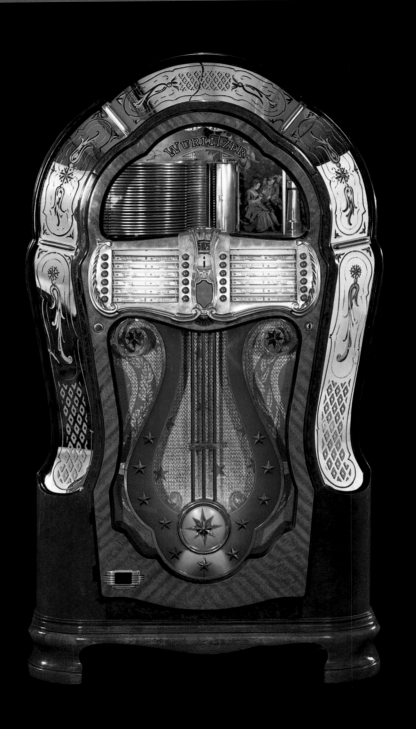

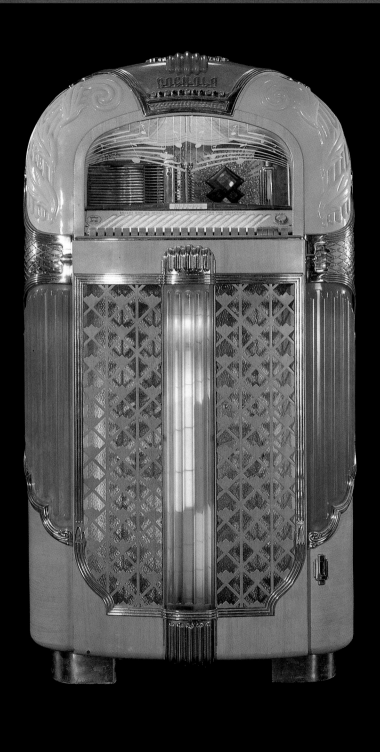

Rock-Ola Model 1428, 1948

• There are hundreds of thousands of small locations in America—a big percentage of which are "naturals" for Wurlitzer Counter Model Phonographs.

Take advantage of this virgin market with Wurlitzer's sensational new Counter Models—Model 41 the smallest Counter Model ever built—

Model 71 the Counter Model with big Console Model features—

Both are complete phonographs with built-in speakers—Glamour Lighting — Visible Record Changers.

Here is a wide-open opportunity to double the size of your operation — to multiply your profits — to test the earning power of locations for the installation of Wurlitzer Console Models later on. The investment required is small — the profit possibilities are large. Now—as when Console Models were first introduced—success depends on *quick action!* Write or wire for details — today!

MODEL 71

TAP THE BIGGEST UNDEVELOPED FIELD IN THE AUTOMATIC MUSIC BUSINESS WITH WURLITZER'S GREAT COUNTER MODELS

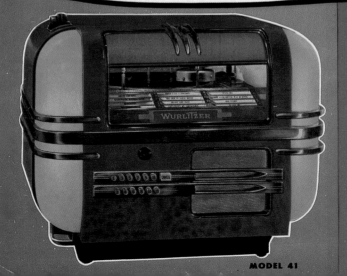

MODEL 41

Cash in!

ON THIS BIG UNDEVELOPED OPPORTUNITY

in Your Locality

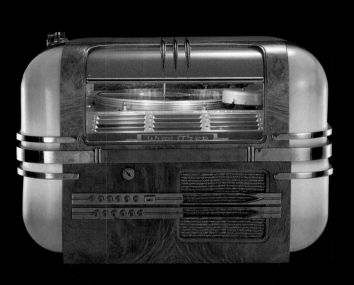

Wurlitzer Model 51, 1937

Wurlitzer Model 61, 1938

Wurlitzer 810 Counter Model Stand, 1942

Install One Or More
WURLITZER WIRELESS BAR BOXES
IN EVERY LOCATION THAT HAS A BAR

Install one or more of these sure-fire money makers in every location that has a bar, fountain or serving counter.

Here crowds congregate and are always in the mood for music. Here you can cash in on Wurlitzer Music as you never did before! Wurlitzer Bar Boxes play every one of the 24 records on the Wurlitzer Phonograph—are attractively finished in polished nickel and walnut burl with red plastic selector knobs. Each has a magnetic coin selector, coin return button and illuminated selector dial. All are equipped with novel built-in clamps for attaching to bars without mutilation.

WURLITZER WIRELESS BAR BOX MODEL 331
Smart looking unit with single illuminated 24 record selector; coin entry in center; program on each side.

WURLITZER WIRELESS BAR BOX MODEL 332

Smallest complete Bar Box made yet it enables patrons to select every one of the 24 records on the Wurlitzer Phonograph.

WURLITZER WIRELESS BAR BOX MODEL 330
A big money maker. Has coin entry and 24 record program selector at each end. Gets the nickels from all directions.

SEE YOUR NEAREST WURLITZER DISTRIBUTOR FOR COMPLETE DETAILS

The Rudolph Wurlitzer Company, North Tonawanda, New York. Canadian Factory: RCA-Victor Co. Ltd., Montreal, Quebec, Canada.

A NAME FAMOUS IN MUSIC FOR OVER TWO HUNDRED YEARS

THE ONLY WIRELESS BAR BOXES THAT ENABLE YOU TO SELECT EVERY RECORD ON THE PHONOGRAPH

SOLD ONLY TO MUSIC MERCHANTS

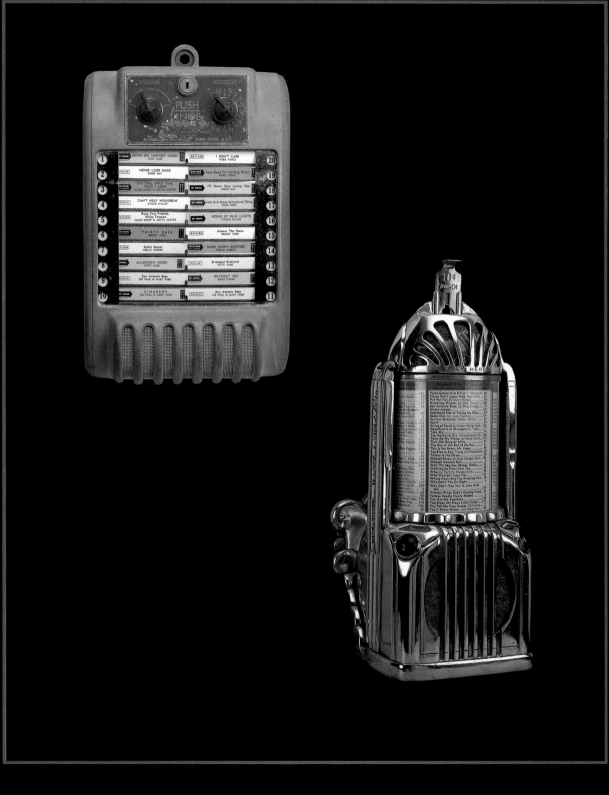

AMI Mighty Midget, 1938

Shyver Multiphone, 1939

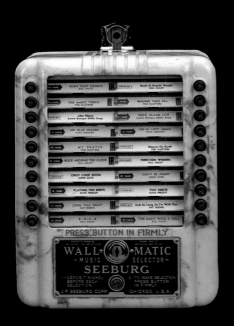

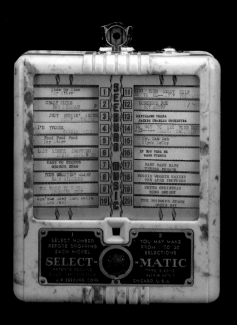

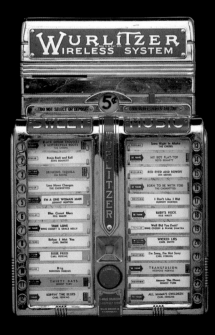

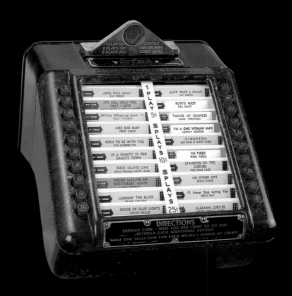

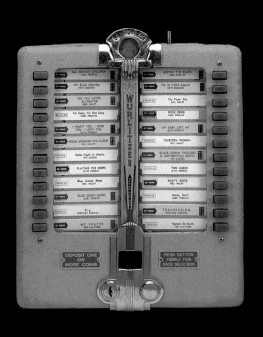

INSERT 5¢ THEN PRESS BUTTON
FIRMLY TO MAKE SELECTIONS

1	ALLEY CAT BENT FABRIC	RAMBLIN' ROSE NAT "KING" COLE	13
2	I REMEMBER YOU FRANK IFIELD	A TASTE OF HONEY MARTIN DENNY	14
3	SHERRY THE FOUR SEASONS	SHEILA TOMMY ROE	15
4	ALL ALONE AM I BRENDA LEE	IT KEEPS RIGHT ON A-HURTIN JOHNNY TILLOTSON	16
5	DEVIL WOMAN MARTY ROBBINS	THE STRIPPER DAVID ROSE	17
6	HERE COMES THAT FEELING BRENDA LEE	GRAVY DEE DEE SHARP	18
7	TWISTIN' AND KISSIN' THE HI-LITES	SNAP YOUR FINGERS JOE HENDERSON	19
8	THE WHITE ROSE OF ATHENS DAVID CARROL	ROSES ARE RED BOBBY VINTON	20
9	SUGAR BLUES ACE CANNON	DON'T BREAK THE HEART CONNIE FRANCIS	21
10	YOU ARE MINE FRANKIE AVALON	YOU DON'T KNOW ME RAY CHARLES	22
11	BABY ELEPHANT WALK LAWRENCE WELK	THINGS BOBBY DARIN	23
12	LONG AS THE ROSE IS RED LORRAINE DARLIN	A LITTLE HEARTACHE EDDY ARNOLD	24

WURLITZER

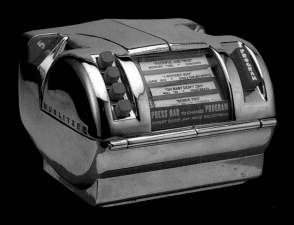

Wurlitzer Model 3045, 1946

Wurlitzer Model 2140 Bar Box, 1948

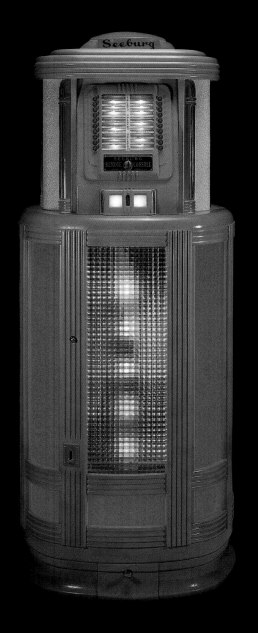

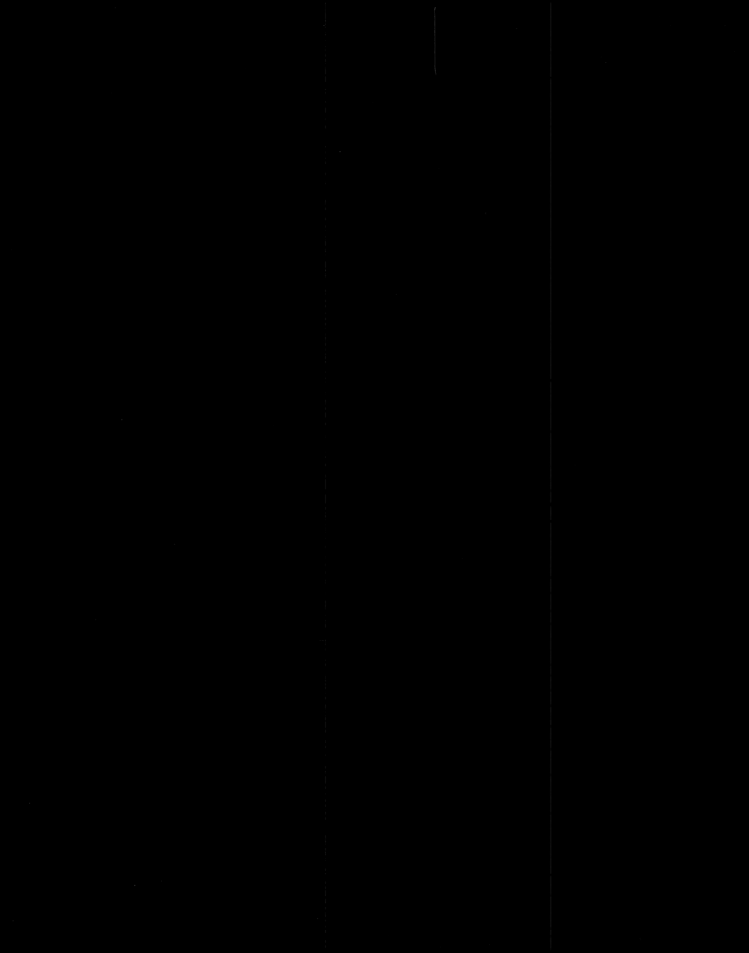

SPEAKERS

WURLITZER MODEL 430
REG. U.S. PAT. OFF.
Selective Organ Speaker

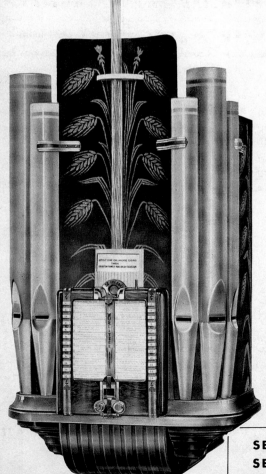

ILLUMINATED PIPE ORGAN PILASTERS

★

5, 10, 25¢ SELECTOR BOX

★

DUAL-WIRE SYSTEM

A fully Selective Speaker with exceptional eye appeal that will attract attention and stimulate phonograph play on its size and brilliance alone.

Constructed of wood veneers with sparkling decorative fabric, illuminated program holder and distinctive illuminated colored pipe organ pilasters, this Model 430 operates on the Dual-Wire System, is extremely easy to mount on any location wall.

Another triumph in the reproduction of Wurlitzer's traditionally fine tone, the Model 430 Selective Speaker reproduces music exactly as the phonograph plays it — rich, clear, inviting extra play from every location patron.

SELECTIVE SPEAKER WITH SELECTOR BOX INSTALLED

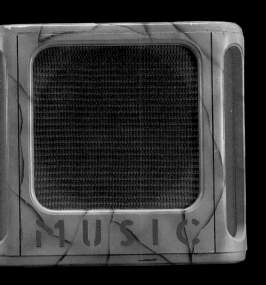

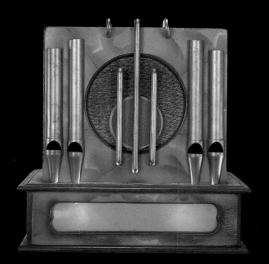

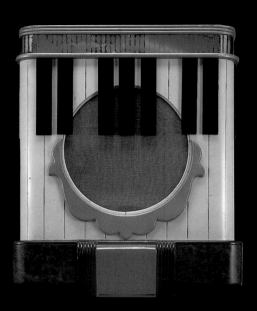

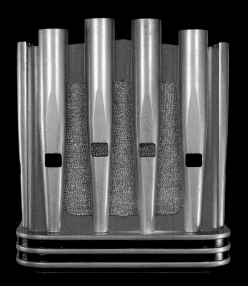
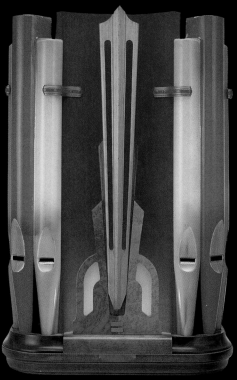

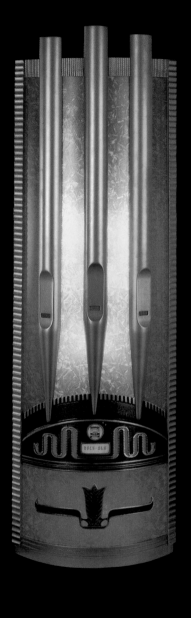

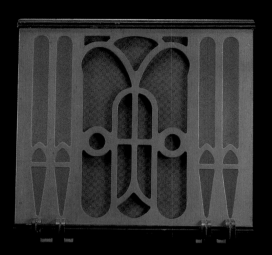

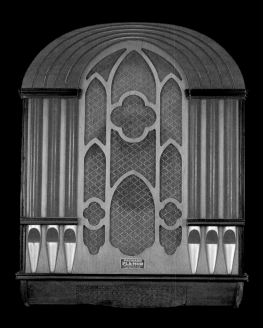

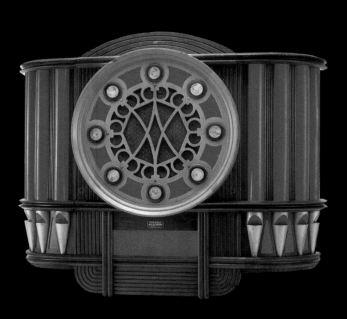

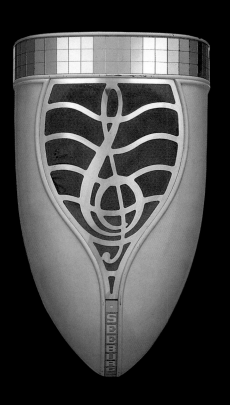

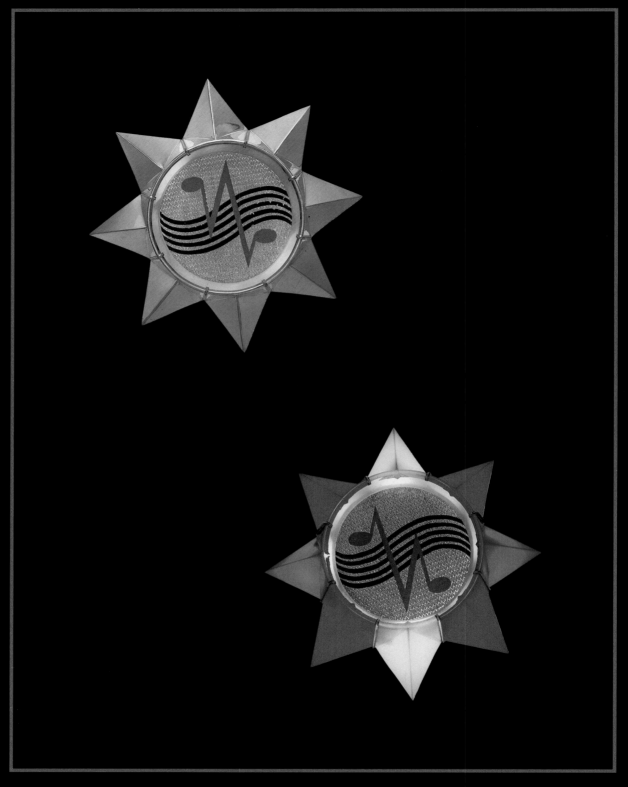

Wurlitzer Model 4000   Wurlitzer Model 4002

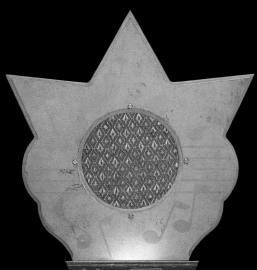

Wurlitzer Model 4005

Wurlitzer Model 4006

Wurlitzer Model 4007

Wurlitzer Model 4008

NOTES

≡ 20 Wurlitzer Model 24, 1938

This 1938 model was released in the fall of 1937. The Model 24 was Wurlitzer's first light-up jukebox and offered 24 selections. It was also the first jukebox to incorporate illuminated plastics in its design. This model represented the company's transition from the heavy wooden radio console cabinets it had used in the past, to a bright and modern deco design that helped establish Wurlitzer's preeminence in the coin-operated phonograph industry. Model 24A had minor mechanical improvements but was cosmetically the same. In all, Wurlitzer shipped 15,000 of these units.
H 52″ × W 31″ × D 25″.

≡ 21 AMI Streamliner, 1938–1940

Manufactured from 1938 to 1940, the Streamliner was one of the first light-up jukeboxes. Its Lumiline incandescent light tube, set behind the vertical center bar in front of the speaker, was a forerunner of the modern fluorescent light. It was the first model sold to the operator and not owned and operated by AMI.
H 52½″ × W 35″ × D 25″.

≡ 22 Wurlitzer Model 500, 1938

The Model 500 was the first jukebox to use rotary color cylinders in the pilasters, and a keyboard selection mechanism. Of the two Wurlitzer models released in August 1938, Models 500 and 600, the 500 was considered the "Deluxe." According to the company's 1938–39 brochure, "Hardest nut for the music merchant to crack has proved to be the white collar and tails type of location frankly and swankly catering to the carriage trade. Few phonographs found welcome in this ultra ultra atmosphere until the advent of the Wurlitzer Deluxe 500." Wurlitzer shipped 15,000 units of this model.
H 58⅝″ × W 35″ × D 28¼″.

≡ 23 Wurlitzer Model 600, 1938

Slightly smaller and less elaborate than the Model 500, this second of Wurlitzer's 1938–39 jukeboxes could be equipped with either a keyboard or rotary selector. The keyboard version had a green arrow that would spin to indicate which of the twenty-four selections was playing. In the rotary model, selector buttons were located in the same place.
H 53⅞″ × W 30⅞″ × D 24⅛″.

≡ 24 Seeburg Classic, 1939

The Seeburg Classic was one of five Symphonola models released in 1939. The others were the Mayfair, Casino, Plaza and Vogue. Only the Classic and Vogue featured the trademark "Marble-Glo" cabinet finish. The Classic was the larger of the two and featured a slightly more powerful sound amplifier.
H 56″ × W 36″ × D 25″.

≡ 25 Mills Throne of Music, 1939

Released the same year as the Mills Empress, the Throne of Music also achieved popularity. At the time, Mills had the most advanced sound systems, but the lack of a visible mechanism was detrimental in stimulating patrons to play the jukebox. Mills released one post-war model, The Constellation, before going bankrupt and being sold to the H. C. Evans Company in 1947.
H 56″ × W 37″ × D 24″.

≡ 26 Seeburg Classic, 1939

True to its name, this 1939 Seeburg model was a representative jukebox for its time. This is another variation on the Classic with a walnut case. Except for the clear glass pilasters flanking the green center strip, the entire body was made of wood and molded plastic. As with most Seeburg models that preceded the M100-A in 1948, the Classic's phonograph mechanism was not visible.
H 56″ × W 36″ × D 25″.

≡ 27 Mills Empress, 1939

Mills Industries, formerly the Mills Novelty Company, was one of the early manufacturers to enter the field with the Dance Master in 1926. The art deco Empress was one of two light-up models released in 1939 and is considered highly collectable. The plastic body was available in four color combinations. Its success increased Mills' percentage of the market share.
H 57″ × W 34″ × D 23″.

≡ 28 Wurlitzer Model 700, 1940

In 1940 and 1941, Paul Fuller designed five distinct full-sized jukeboxes in a series that included the Models 700, 750, 800 and 850. Wurlitzer sold 9,498 of the 700, the economy model of the 1940 line. The company's glowing promotional copy read, "On the Model 700, pilasters of rich Italian onyx may be illumi-

nated either by using bulbs of varying colors to attain a rich blending of shades, or by using bulbs of a single color to match the predominant note of the location's decorator scheme . . . another Wurlitzer triumph in glamour lighting."
H 56½" × W 32" × D 25½".

≡ 29 Seeburg Envoy, 1940

The Envoy was in a group of similar full-sized boxes manufactured by Seeburg in 1940, which included the Cadet, Major, Colonel, Commander and Concert Master. The Envoy featured an airbrushed base and marbleized plastic. Glass rods flanked the central green plastic pilaster in front of the speaker.
H 59½" × W 36½" × D 24½".

≡ 30 Wurlitzer Model 800, 1940

The last of Wurlitzer's exclusively mechanical selection jukeboxes, the 1940 deluxe Model 800 featured three bubble tubes in its center pilasters and the longest color cylinders Wurlitzer ever used, surrounding incandescent bulbs in its side pilasters. Light from a rotating color cylinder was broken by zebra-striped acetate on the back of the pilaster making it flicker like fire. The production run was 11,501 units.
H 61" × W 37" × D 27¾".

≡ 31 Rock-Ola Master Rockolite, 1941

The 1941 Model 1403 Master Rockolite jukebox was distinguished from its predecessor, the 1940 Model 1401 Master walnut phonograph, by its faux-marble cabinet treatment. This was one of the Luxury Light-Up series Rock-Ola produced from 1939 through 1941. The Master was slightly smaller than its more elaborate companion jukebox, the Super, which was released at the same time.
H 52" × W 33¼" × D 24½".

≡ 32 Wurlitzer Model 750, 1941

Wurlitzer shipped 18,411 units of the Model 750 and its variation, the 750-E (with electric keyboard selector). They were the most popular of Wurlitzer's 1941 jukeboxes. They featured two small, curved, bubble tubes beneath the selector buttons, and a choice of either a mural or an illuminated back door behind the record-changing mechanism. Its convenient size,

smaller than the other Wurlitzer models, contributed to its success.
H 55¾" × W 32" × D 26".

≡ 33 Seeburg 9800, 1941

Like Rock-Ola's Spectravox and AMI's Singing Towers, the speaker of the 9800 was mounted horizontally. The sound was bounced against the face of a concealed metal wedge that projected the music throughout the room. This 1941 box had a single color cylinder located behind the glass door in the front. It featured "Fountain of Light" cabinet illumination and glass "candlelight" upper pilasters.
H 66¾" × W 37⅜" × D 27¾".

≡ 34 Wurlitzer Model 780, 1941

The 780 was one of two Colonials produced by Wurlitzer. The Model 1080 of 1947 was the other. Wurlitzer's 1941 brochure explains that it is "styled to harmonize with the finest furnishings. Early American from its Governor Winthrop cabinet to its pewter finished hardware; from its spinning wheel grille with colorful patchwork background to its butterfly peg construction, the rich conservative beauty of this instrument marks a decided departure from the 'commercial' appearance of all other automatic phonographs."
H 61" × W 37¾" × D 25½".

≡ 35 AMI Singing Towers, 1941

This 20-selection model was introduced in 1940 as a 1941 model and sold until the spring of 1942. Its speaker was mounted horizontally in the top of the cabinet. As a result, the sound reflected off the glass dome top and radiated throughout the room. Except for the plastic program selector bars, everything transparent on this box was three-quarter-inch glass including the top dome.
H 70" × W 36" × D 25".

≡ 36 Wurlitzer Model 850, 1941

"The only super deluxe phonograph in the industry" is the way Wurlitzer described the 1941 Model 850. It was considered Paul Fuller's greatest triumph in design. Known as the Peacock, it used polarized films and an analyzer to generate color in the Peacock glass. As a result of this innovation, advertisements at the time of its release proclaimed that there was "Nothing like it ever on any phonograph." This statement is

still true today. Wurlitzer shipped 10,002 of these extraordinary machines, and 456 of the Model 850-A.
H 65½″ × W 39″ × D 26½″.

≡ 37 Rock-Ola Spectravox, 1941

After a coin was deposited, the selection on the 1941 Spectravox "Tone Column" was dialed as if dialing a telephone. The music came out the top—under the bowl, which acted as a sound deflector and "showered" music over the patrons. It was an elaborate remote selector unit with a speaker. It could be used with a Rock-Ola jukebox located in another part of the room, or with the 1411 Play Master unit. The Play Master contained the phonograph mechanism and power amplification and could be located where convenient. The surface of the Spectravox was painted to look like wood grain. Corrugated steel running up the center and sides reflected the red illuminated plastic.
H 84½″ × W 28″ × D 28″.

≡ 38 Wurlitzer Model 950, 1942

When the United States went to war, jukebox manufacturers reduced production of coin-operated music machines and retooled for wartime production. As a result, only 3,497 of the Model 950 were shipped in 1942, making it the most collectable jukebox of the era. This design was the forerunner of the most popular jukebox of all time, the 1946 Model 1015. Because metal was in short supply as production on this box began, many of its internal components, including the coin chutes, coin box and tone arm post, were made of wood. Glass was also substituted for plastic in some cases.
H 61¾″ × W 36⁹/₁₆″ × D 25⅞″.

≡ 39 Rock-Ola Commando, 1942

Because plastic use was restricted during the war, all the transparent parts of this rare 1942 jukebox were glass except the three red panels in the bottom section. The lower casing was bird's-eye maple. The Commando's record-changing mechanism, like that of the Master Rockolite, was not visible to the patron. Four separate doors in the front of the box opened to allow the operator to repair the machine or change its records. It was the last of a series of three similar models. The other two were the Model 1413 Premier and the elaborate Model 1414 President.
H 72¼″ × W 33″ × D 25½″.

≡ 40 Wurlitzer Victory Cabinet, 1942–1945

As a result of the suspension of jukebox manufacturing due to the war, Wurlitzer shipped 18,000 Victory cabinets between 1942 and 1945. It was designed to house the components of the Wurlitzer models 24, 500, 600, 700 and 800 of the pre-war era. There were two primary variations, the rotary selector and the keyboard selector; the latter is shown here.
H 65½″ × W 41″ × D 27″.

≡ 41 Rock-Ola Model 1422, 1946

Model 1422 was the first of three in the Magic-Glo series of boxes manufactured by Rock-Ola immediately after the war in 1946. It had two color cylinders lit by incandescent bulbs behind its wooden grille, two more in its side pilasters lit by fluorescent tubes, and shoulders lit by more incandescent bulbs. A stylized eighteenth-century European courting scene was silk-screened on the paper backdrop, surrounding the chrome-plated record stack on three sides.
H 58″ × W 29¾″ × D 26″.

≡ 42 AMI Model A, Mother of Plastic, 1946

The 1946 Model A, also known as the Mother of Plastic, was the first jukebox to make extensive use of acrylic plastics, and the first to use colored fluorescent lights. Two color cylinders, one on either side of the base of the box, were activated when the motor started, so that insertion of a coin bought animated lights with your musical selection. Leading the competition with 40-selection capability, 11,200 of the Model A were sold through 1947.
H 72″ × W 37½″ × D 25¾″.

≡ 43 Wurlitzer Model 1015, 1946

With animated color in the side pilasters, new die casting, three-dimensional plastics, and bubble tubes running from its base to its arch, the Model 1015 was the most popular jukebox of all time. The 1015 was on the drawing board prior to the war, designed to follow the Model 950 in late 1942 or 1943. Wurlitzer shipped 56,000 1015s in 1946 and 1947, accompanied by the largest promotional campaign in jukebox history, including swizzle sticks, napkins, tabletops, coasters, decals, billboards and prominent advertisements in national magazines, all proclaiming "Wurlitzer is Music!"
H 59⅞″ × W 33½″ × D 25″.

≡ **44 Packard Pla-Mor Manhattan, 1946**
The 1946 Packard Manhattan was the deluxe model of the two full-sized, high-quality jukeboxes produced by Homer E. Capehart while he served as a United States senator (R–Indiana). The cabinet was made of burled wood, the window was etched glass, the mechanism was completely chromed; black musical notes were screened onto yellow glass inside the cabinet. The Manhattan played one side of each of 24 disks. Packard produced 14,830 of this model.
H 61 5/8″ × W 25 15/16″ × D 24 1/8″.

≡ **45 Filben Maestro, 1946**
In an attempt to cash in on tremendous post-war demand for coin-operated phonographs, Filben produced the Maestro between 1946 and 1948. It was a 30-selection 78 rpm jukebox. Prior to 1946 Filben manufactured mirror cabinets and "Hideaway" units only. It was the only full-sized jukebox Filben ever produced.
H 56″ × W 32″ × D 28″.

≡ **46 Seeburg Model 147, 1947**
The 20-selection Model 147 was the second post-war release from Seeburg. It was part of their Barrel series updated through 1948. It had a wooden or metal cabinet with a white dome and color wheel, red pilasters and an excellent sound system. In spite of this, it didn't fare well, because the mechanism couldn't be seen.
H 57″ × W 36″ × D 26 1/2″.

≡ **47 Wurlitzer Ambassador Kit, 1947**
The Ambassador kit was designed to give the Wurlitzer Model 1015 a new look. It is one example of the many after-market kits used to "modernize" jukeboxes. The use of kits to remodel old coin-operated phonographs reached its peak during the war years, due to high demand and scarcity caused by wartime restriction of production.
H 59 7/8″ × W 33 1/2″ × D 25″.

≡ **48 Rock-Ola Model 1426, 1947**
The 1947 Rock-Ola 1426, second in the Magic-Glo series, was similar to its predecessor, the Model 1422. The primary features that distinguished it were that the center strip in front of the speaker was metal instead of wood; the grille lit up in five colors rather than four; only two color cylinders were used in the side pilasters and there were none behind the grille; and the mural

behind the record-changing mechanism was a quilted gold cloth with jeweled mirrors. Rock-Ola also used a lively musical motif in the phonograph window.
H 58″ × W 29 3/4″ × D 26″.

≡ **49 Packard Pla-Mor Model 7, 1947**
This Pla-Mor was Packard's economy model for 1947. Small, incandescent bulbs illuminated radically deep molded red plastics. A musical motif, screened onto sheet plastic, backed a complex changer mechanism that kicked the selection from a horizontal stack and passed it to a second record holder, which placed the disc on the turntable. Like the Manhattan, the Model 7 played one side each of 24 records, selected on the unique Packard wheel. The production run was 9,810.
H 62 1/2″ × W 35″ × D 26 1/4″.

≡ **50 Wurlitzer Colonial, Model 1080, 1947**
This 1947–48 model contained all the mechanical refinements of the earlier Model 1015. Wurlitzer also produced a Model 1080-A, which was cosmetically identical to the 1080, but contained the Model 1100 sound system. The Colonial, like the pre-war Model 780, was designed to appeal to more conservative locations.
H 58 5/8″ × W 33 3/4″ × D 25″.

≡ **51 AMI Model B, 1948**
The AMI Model B was a toned-down version of the Model A. Released in 1948, it had the same mechanism as the models A and C, which played 40 selections on 20 discs. It used two color wheels in the lower pilasters, and a third in the upper pilaster. The cabinet was available in "Bisque Blond" or "Sheraton Mahogany," which is depicted here. AMI shipped 8,430 of this model until 1950, when they introduced the Model C.
H 64″ × W 33″ × D 24″.

≡ **52 Seeburg Model 148, 1948**
Following Models 146 (1946) and 147 (1947), this 1948 model was the third and rarest in a series of three jukeboxes with identical bodies known as the "Trash Can" or the "Barrel." It was distinguished from its predecessors by its blonde wood-grained metal cabinet and its fluted white dome. The 148 was the only box of

the three to use a color cylinder in its dome and another in the bottom of its grille.
H 57″ × W 36″ × D 26½″.

≡ 53 Rock-Ola Model 1428, 1948
Model 1428 of 1948 was the last of the Magic-Glo series released by Rock-Ola. Mechanically, it was the same as its predecessors, Models 1422 and 1426. A blonde wood-grained finish was painted on the metal front door. The ruby side and green top pilasters were illuminated, and the animated color wheel behind the central plastic grille spilled changing colors onto the reflective grille cloth.
H 58″ × W 29¾″ × D 26″.

≡ 54 Wurlitzer Model 1100, 1948
After the success of its Model 1015, Wurlitzer miscalculated the demand for this last jukebox designed by Paul Fuller. Only 16,200 were produced and many were returned or never left the assembly line. This 1948–49 model was the first jukebox to use a lightweight plastic "Cobra" tone arm. It required the first use of a pre-amp in jukebox history. Its mechanical innovations reduced record wear while improving fidelity. The selector bar rotated when pressed, offering the patron a view of eight selections at a time, numbered 1–8, 9–16 and 17–24.
H 56½″ × W 30″ × D 25¼″.

TABLE MODELS

≡ 56 Wurlitzer Model 50, 1937
The 1937 12-selection Model 50 was a small console for locations with limited floor space. The cabinet was finished in African mahogany veneer. Its Lucite grille rods were colored with amber gels that allowed light to shoot through the plastic on the exposed sides. Its back door mural was three-dimensional, made of painted wooden half-rounds. The production run was 1,180 units.
H 47½″ × W 23¼″ × D 17⁷⁄₁₆″.

≡ 57 Rock-Ola Model CM39, 1939
Rock-Ola devoted its effort to full-sized jukeboxes, telephones and remote systems. This 1939 Luxury Light-Up model was one of only two table units the company

made; the other was the Junior model released in 1940. Both required a remote speaker because Rock-Ola countertop models did not contain one.
H 22⅝″ × W 24″ × D 21″.

≡ 58 Wurlitzer Model 41, 1940
Wurlitzer produced 2,010 units in 1940–41 of the Model 41. It featured myrtle burl veneer and amber catalin plastic pilasters on the front and rear. This model opened for servicing at the center metal bar. It is the smallest jukebox ever made.
H 17″ × W 21¼″ × D 18⅞″.

≡ 59 Wurlitzer Model 51, 1937
The Model 51 was the only Wurlitzer table model made without illuminated plastics. Manufactured in 1937, its wooden African mahogany veneer reflected the jukebox design that preceded the light-up era of the early to mid-thirties. Wurlitzer produced 1,200 units of this model.
H 20″ × W 27½″ × D 18½″.

≡ 60 Wurlitzer Model 61, 1938
Wurlitzer produced 8,260 of this model, making it the most common of all the classic Wurlitzer table models. It featured maple and walnut veneers with wood-grained metal escutcheons on the upper half of its case, and illuminated red plastic corners. It was released in August 1938 as a 1939 model.
H 22″ × W 21¼″ × D 18″.

≡ 61 Wurlitzer Model 71, 1940
The Model 71 featured myrtle burl and straight-grained walnut veneers with amber and red illuminated plastics in a wooden cabinet. Wurlitzer shipped 4,506 units between 1940 and 1941. The company shipped 913 units of their last counter model, the 81, in 1942 (not shown). It was identical in every way to the Model 71 except for the substitution of marbleized amber for clear amber plastics in the side pilasters, and a different walnut veneer.
H 23⅛″ × W 21¼″ × D 18″.

≡ 62 Wurlitzer 410 Counter Model Stand, 1942
The 1941 Model 410 stand was designed for the Wurlitzer Counter Model 41. It was an adaptation of the Model 710 stand which accommodated counter models 61, 71 and 81. The back of the stand could be

removed for additional storage of records. It was offered as a free premium with the purchase of a table model.
H 36" × W 21½" × D 21½".

≡ **63 Wurlitzer 810 Counter Model Stand, 1942**
The 810 counter model stand, displayed here with the Model 71, was designed by Paul Fuller to accommodate Wurlitzer Models 61, 71 and 81. It combined transfer reproductions of oriental walnut, rosewood, redwood and myrtle burl veneers with decorative maple veneer inlays.
H 34¾" × W 24⅛" × D 19".

WALL BOXES

≡ **66 Seeburg Play-Boy, 1939**
The 1939 Seeburg Play-boy was a portable "wireless" remote selection unit. It contained its own volume control and speaker. It was designed to operate the Master Seeburg Symphonola jukebox by plugging into an ordinary A/C receptacle.
H 40" × W 16½" × D 15".

≡ **67 AMI Mighty Midget, 1938**   (Top)
On January 1, 1938, AMI made history when the company released the first wall box, the Mighty Midget. Complete with speaker, it echoed the design of the Streamliner model released the same year. The other manufacturers immediately followed suit.
H 14½" × W 8¼" × D 4".

≡ **67 Shyver Multiphone, 1939**   (Bottom)
The Shyver Multiphone was a music selection device that operated over telephone lines in Seattle, Tacoma and Olympia, Washington, from 1939 to 1959. A patron could deposit a coin and speak with a telephone operator seated at a turntable, who would then play a selection, which would be played from a speaker in the bottom of the selection device. Originally it was introduced at five cents per play and later increased to ten cents per play.
H 16¾" × W 6¼" × D 6¼".

≡ **68 Seeburg Wall-O-Matic, 1940**   (Top)
The 1940 nickel-only Seeburg wireless Model WS-2Z Wall-O-Matic was compatible only with Seeburg equipment.
H 12½" × W 8⅝" × D 4¾".

≡ **68 Wurlitzer Model 310, 1940**   (Bottom)
The 1940 illuminated Model 310 was the first wall selector unit Wurlitzer produced.
H 14⅜" × W 9⅛" × D 4⅝".

≡ **69 Seeburg Select-O-Matic, 1940**   (Top)
The 1940 Seeburg Model 520-1Z Select-O-Matic was designed to work not only with 20-selection Seeburg jukeboxes, but adaptor kits were available for 16 or 24 selections to be used with Wurlitzer equipment as well.
H 11½" × W 8½" × D 3½".

≡ **69 Wurlitzer Model 320, 1940**   (Bottom)
This 1940 Wurlitzer Model 320 wall box had the rare Model 360 wireless impulse transmitter option.
H 10 9/16" × W 9¼" × D 4".

≡ **70 Seeburg Melody Parade, 1940**   (Top)
The tiny 1940 Seeburg Bakelite Model MS-1Z Melody Parade wireless remote selector featured the five most popular selections from twenty found on the jukebox.
H 4⅛" × W 5" × D 7".

≡ **70 Seeburg Bar-O-Matic, 1940**   (Bottom)
Seeburg's Model WB-1Z Bakelite Bar-O-Matic was introduced in 1940. This three-wire remote control selector came with a choice of 5-10-25 cent coin entry.
H 9" × W 9¼" × D 10½".

≡ **71 Wurlitzer Model 331 Bar Box, 1940**   (Top)
The 1940 Wurlitzer Model 331 Bar Box was designed to be clamped on with no damage to the surface. Its low profile was a selling feature because it wouldn't interfere with the serving of drinks and couldn't be knocked over. The cash box was located under the bar.
H 5⅛" × W 25¾" × D 4½".

≡ **71 Wurlitzer Model 100, 1941**   (Bottom)
The Wurlitzer Model 100 was a 30-wire wall box that only accepted nickels. It was released in late 1941.
H 9¼" × W 9" × D 4".

≡ **72 Wurlitzer Model 120, 1941** (Top)
The 1941 Wurlitzer Model 120 was a two-wire wall box that only accepted nickels.
H 9¹⁵/₁₆″ × W 10″ × D 4½″.

≡ **72 Packard Butler, 1940** (Bottom)
The Butler was available in a satin or chrome finish with a five or ten cent coin drop. A patron turned the red side dials to a selection and then deposited the coin.
H 10¾″ × W 7¾″ × D 6¼″.

≡ **73 Wurlitzer Model 125, 1942** (Top)
The 1942 Model 125 Wurlitzer wall box featured amber plastic.
H 12½″ × W 10¼″ × D 5″.

≡ **73 Wurlitzer Model 125, 1942** (Bottom)
The 1942 Wurlitzer Model 125 metal wall box featured a painted wood grain and red pin striping. It was released after the amber plastic version.
H 12½″ × W 10¼″ × D 5″.

≡ **74 Wurlitzer Model 125, 1942** (Top)
This Wurlitzer Model 125 wall box featured a yellow Acme Sales wrinkle-finish replacement cover. This after-market cover was used to replace the amber plastic Model 125 fronts which had a tendency to shrink a great deal from the heat of the internal light bulb, and, as a result, were easily vandalized.
H 12½″ × W 10¼″ × D 5″.

≡ **74 Wurlitzer 430 Wall Box, 1942** (Bottom)
This wall box is from the Wurlitzer Model 430 speaker, which was a two-wire remote speaker and selector. At the end of the speaker's production run the wall boxes were available individually.
H 12½″ × W 10¼″ × D 5″.

≡ **75 Wurlitzer Model 3020, 1946** (Top)
The Model 3020, a three-wire wall box, was produced in 1946 and used with the Wurlitzer Models 1015, 1080 and 1100 jukeboxes. It accepted nickels, dimes and quarters.
H 11¾″ × W 8⅞″ × D 5¹¹/₁₆″.

≡ **75 Wurlitzer Model 3031, 1946** (Bottom)
The Wurlitzer Model 3031, "one of the smallest and simplest units ever built," was a less expensive 30-wire unit that accepted only nickels and was used with the post-war models 1015 and 1080 jukeboxes.
H 9″ × W 7½″ × D 4⅜″.

≡ **76 Wurlitzer Model 3045, 1946** (Top)
The wireless Model 3045 was produced in 1946 by Wurlitzer to accompany the models 1015 and 1080 jukeboxes.
H 11¾″ × W 8⅞″ × D 5¹¹/₁₆″.

≡ **76 Wurlitzer Model 2140 Bar Box, 1948** (Bottom)
The Model 2140, nicknamed "the Frog," was the smallest bar box Wurlitzer ever built. It accepted five and ten cent coins, but could be converted to take a dime or a quarter per play with the kit #88. It was used in conjunction with the Wurlitzer Model 1100 jukebox of 1948.
H 5⅜″ × W 7⅝″ × D 7½″.

≡ **77 Seeburg Duo-Remote Console, 1942**
The 1942 Seeburg Duo-Remote Console Model WC-1Z is another pre-war example of a "stroller" with a remote speaker. It featured illuminated red plastics and a "fountain of light animated color display" in the quilted bottom door glass.
H 59½″ × W 36½″ × D 24½″.

S P E A K E R S

P R E - W A R   S P E A K E R S

≡ **80 Seeburg Deluxe Illuminated Extra Speaker** (Top)
This 1938 Seeburg "Marble-Glo" speaker was called the "Deluxe Illuminated Extra Speaker." Seeburg's first internally illuminated speaker could be used with all models for the 1938–39 line. Priced at $15, it came equipped with its own volume control and 50 feet of extension wire.
H 16½″ × W 17¾″ × D 11¼″.

≡ **80 Wurlitzer Model 160** (Bottom)
The Model 160 came with a neutral finish or maple veneer. Wurlitzer designed this auxiliary speaker to complement the full-sized Model 780, the Wagon Wheel. This "colonial" speaker was intended to suit a wide va-

riety of locations ". . . because of its conservative styling and design."
H 28″ × W 19⅛″ × D 10¼″.

≡ 81 **Wurlitzer Model 210**   (Top)
Similar to the Model 220 except for its flat top, this speaker had a wooden case with wooden bars that reached horizontally across the speaker cloth. At the base, the illuminated plastic grille was emblazoned with the Wurlitzer logo.
H 17″ × W 16¼″ × D 7¾″.

≡ 81 **Wurlitzer Model 220**   (Bottom)
The plastic "Music" plate was the only illuminated part of this wooden speaker. Both the 210 and 220 resembled the radio cabinet styling of the pre-war era.
H 16″ × W 14⅛″ × D 7¾″.

≡ 82 **Rock-Ola Pre-War Speaker**   (Top)
This pre-war Rock-Ola speaker from 1941 featured a faux-marble finish with golden organ pipes and an illuminated red plastic base.
H 21¼″ × W 20¾″ × D 12″.

≡ 82 **Kleertone**   (Bottom)
Kleertone remote speakers were manufactured in Evansville, Indiana. They had several models and could be used with any jukebox. Higher model numbers indicated larger speaker cabinets.
H 21″ × W 19″ × D 9″.

≡ 83 **Kleertone Model 125**   (Top)
The Kleertone Model 125 is a pre-war extension speaker adaptable to any jukebox of the era.
H 27½″ × W 23½″ × D 11¼″.

≡ 83 **Wurlitzer Model 39-A**   (Bottom)
The case of the Model 39-A was finished in walnut veneer. The nameplates at top and bottom and red side plastics were illuminated. The lettering on the Model 39 said, "Music by / Wurlitzer," rather than "Strike Up the Band / Wurlitzer."
H 7¾″ × 17⅜″ diameter.

≡ 84 **Wurlitzer Model 250**   (Top)
The Model 250's cabinet featured walnut and burl maple veneers. The red grille bars were painted wood, and "Music by Wurlitzer" was illuminated. The speaker

was manufactured in two versions. The 250 was hard wired to the jukebox, and the other—the 350, identical in appearance—employed a "wireless" transformer, which allowed it to operate by plugging into an ordinary A/C receptacle.
H 27¼″ × W 21″ × D 11⅝″.

≡ 84 **Seeburg Top Spot**   (Bottom)
Produced in 1940–41, the Seeburg Top Spot speaker was designed to accompany the very rare Concert Master jukebox which featured the same comedy and tragedy masks in its design.
H 23″ × W 23″ × D 11¼″.

≡ 85 **Seeburg Speak-O-Gram**   (Top)
This was one of many variations of the Seeburg Speak-O-Gram series that used the pre-war organ pipe motif. Most had an illuminated plastic panel at the base that spilled light upon the lower portion of the grille cloth and organ pipes. Other models used faux-marble finish termed by Seeburg as "Marble-Glo." The company made many versions of the Speak-O-Gram; most included organ pipes in some configuration. The organ pipes were strictly cosmetic, since the speaker itself was placed behind the center grille in these pre-war units. It was intended to provide auxiliary sound for the Models 146, 147 and 148 as well as pre-war models.

≡ 85 **Wurlitzer Model 420**   (Bottom)
The Model 420 was a wall-mounted remote speaker produced in 1942. An identical Model 421 was wireless. Its pilasters were made of glass because of the shortage of plastic during the war. It was very similar to the Model 430, but contained no selection unit. The production run was approximately 700.
H 42¼″ × W 23″ × D 14⁵⁄₁₆″.

≡ 86 **Rock-Ola Organ Type**   (Top)
Rock-Ola produced two auxiliary corner speakers as part of the Tone Column series it released in 1941. The Model 1806 Organ Speaker was designed to be suspended in the corner of a room so that the walls on either side would reflect sound into the room. The speaker was located in the top of the cabinet. It was touted in its brochure as ". . . easily the most eye and ear-filling object in a location."
H 63″ × W 19½″ × D 15¾″.

≡ **86 Rock-Ola Moderne** (Bottom)
The other 1941 Rock-Ola Moderne corner speaker, featured an illuminated central "Chromed Tone Column" that housed the speaker and lighting. The lights illuminated the amber plastic and red side plastic which reflected on the concave chrome ribbed interior curve. Between the severe contemporary lines of the Moderne and the warm traditional design of the Organ, Rock-Ola hoped to cover a wide range of locations.
H 57½″ × W 18¾″ × D 17″.

≡ **87 Wurlitzer Model 430** (Top)
Manufactured in 1942, this last in Wurlitzer's pre-war line of speakers was intended to accompany the full-sized Model 950. It was a wall selector unit with a built-in speaker. The cash drawer was concealed in the base. Very few of these speakers survived through the years with their glass pilasters intact. The production run was approximately 2000.
H 46¹⁵⁄₁₆″ × W 23″ × D 14⁵⁄₁₆″.

≡ **87 Wurlitzer Model 580** (Bottom)
Perhaps the loveliest of all auxiliary speaker units, with quilted maple and walnut veneers, the large Model 580 was the only speaker ever to have bubble tubes, which made up its flower stems. The bubble-tubed design was echoed in the Wurlitzer Model 850-A. In that full-size model this design was substituted for the polarizing peacock glass. Only 456 of the Model 850-A were produced. Although it was a wall unit, the Model 580 was actually taller and wider than the petite Wurlitzer Model 50 floor console. Approximately 960 of these speakers were produced.
H 49⅝″ × W 33″ × D 14⅜″.

≡ **88 and 89 Packard Pre-War Speakers**
The Packard Manufacturing Company made a wide selection of remote speakers in various shapes and sizes to fit the needs of specific locations. In the pre-war period, their primary interest was remote selection systems and "hideaway" units. They did not produce full-size freestanding jukeboxes until after World War II.
88 H 17″ × W 17¾″ × D 8¾″.   (Top)
88 H 29½″ × W 23½″ × D 10½″.   (Bottom)
89 H 42″ × W 50″ × D 13″.

≡ **90 Seeburg Teardrop** (Top)
Seeburg introduced the large Mirror model auxiliary wall speaker in 1946. It was almost 36 inches high and contained a 12-inch permanent magnet speaker. Production ceased with the introduction of the Model M100-A jukebox in December of 1948. The much smaller 8-inch Teardrop speaker introduced at the same time had more longevity. It was produced through the 1950s.

≡ **90 Rock-Ola Tonette** (Bottom)
The Rock-Ola Tonette, Model 1606, was a small auxiliary speaker. It featured straight-grain walnut veneer and a deco design Bakelite grille.
H 14″ × W 10½″ × D 6¼″.

≡ **91 Rock-Ola Tone-O-Lier** (Top)
This was one of two Tone-O-Lier chandelier type speakers that Rock-Ola produced in the post-war era. The fixture was intended to hang from the ceiling, the speaker facing down so that sound would radiate into the room. A color cylinder inside the case revolved, changing the colors of the side panels.
H 15½″ × 23″ diameter.

≡ **91 Packard Rose** (Bottom)
The Model 900, the "Rose," was first released in 1946 by Packard. It was one of three hammertone steel body speakers that introduced a new post-war contemporary look, a departure from the warm furniture quality of the pre-war models.
H 28″ × W 23½″ × D 11¼″.

≡ **92 Packard Lily** (Top)
The Model 950 was known as the Lily. The Orchid, the Iris and the Lily were a group of speakers released by Packard in 1948, similar in look and descending in size. These models echoed the styling that was Packard's design signature in the pre-war era.
H 22⅞″ × W 22″ × D 9¾″.

≡ **92 Packard Iris** (Bottom)
The Model 1100 was described in Packard's 1948 brochure as follows: "The 'Iris,' in Packard's new speaker

design, is a pleasing pattern of polished woods decorated with panels of colored molded plastic. Both front and sides are brilliantly illuminated. New beauty of tone and performance is achieved through the use of wood for cabinets and by obtaining the finest speakers possible for reproducing every note with high fidelity."
H 27⅞" × W 28⅜" × D 11¼".

≡ **93 Filben Teardrop**
The Filben Teardrop remote speaker closely resembled Seeburg's post-war designs. The cast aluminum speaker case was painted red to match their Maestro full-sized jukebox.
H 17" × W 11" × D 6".

Wurlitzer Post-War Speakers

≡ **94 Wurlitzer Model 4000**   (Top)
The Model 4000 was a nickel-plated star speaker. When lit it would project a star light pattern on the wall or ceiling behind it. The Models 4000, 4002 and 4004 featured eight-inch permanent magnet speakers.
H 8¼" × 23¾" diameter.

≡ **94 Wurlitzer Model 4002**   (Bottom)
This speaker was identical to the Model 4000, except for the illuminated plastics that replaced the metal star. Both had two grille cloth options available. One was a nickel-plated eight-point star, and the other had a silk-screened, flocked Wurlitzer "W" on a staff of wavy musical lines.
H 8¼" × 23¾" diameter.

≡ **95 Wurlitzer Model 4003**   (Top)
The all-wood-frame Model 4003 was painted bone white and trimmed in gold. The notes and the grille cloth were silver. The neutral colors enabled the speaker to take on the color of the light bulb the owner chose depending on the house's color scheme.
H 20¼" × W 17½" × D 6¾".

≡ **95 Wurlitzer Model 4004**   (Bottom)
The "Johnny One-Note" logo, illuminated from behind, was prominently displayed in red plastic on the Model

4004. The black and golden yellow parts were painted metal. The Models 4003, 4004, 4005 and 4006 all featured eight-inch permanent magnet speakers with three-and-one-half inch voice coils.
H 7¾" × 16½" diameter.

≡ **96 Wurlitzer Model 4005**   (Top)
The Model 4005 was an inexpensive yet attractive non-illuminated all-wood walnut speaker. The grille cloth had another variation on the combination of the Wurlitzer "W" with musical notes and staff lines. It had excellent fidelity due to the new "SonoCircle" tone chamber.
H 6" × 16½" diameter.

≡ **96 Wurlitzer Model 4006**   (Bottom)
The Model 4006 was a round mirrored speaker trimmed in red with an inner gold circle surrounding the grille cloth. "Wurlitzer Music" was painted on the radiating reflective mirror face. It also featured the exclusive "SonoCircle" tone chamber.
H 8" × 19" diameter.

≡ **97 Wurlitzer Model 4007**   (Top)
The large oval design of the Model 4007 accommodated a 12-inch speaker and featured "everchanging colors" that played on the silver metallic grille cloth and mirrored rim. These originated from the moving color wheel located behind the three-dimensional logo of "Johnny One-Note" in the translucent plastic Wurlitzer nameplate, on the bottom face of the speaker.
H 30½" × W 22¾" × D 11⅝".

≡ **97 Wurlitzer Model 4008**   (Bottom)
The Model 4008 was the most elaborate speaker produced in the post-war period and was the first 15-inch auxiliary speaker ever offered. This was the same size as the speaker in the phonograph and its sound reproduction quality was excellent. It could be mounted either on the ceiling or on the wall. It was mirrored on the concave interior surface, and at the center hub, a color wheel tinted the mirrors as it revolved. The red, yellow and green plastic parts were also illuminated. The use of polished aluminum escutcheons echoed the design of the full-sized Model 1015.
H 16⁷⁄₁₆" × 32⅛" diameter.

ACKNOWLEDGMENTS

The jukeboxes in this book are from the collections of the following individuals. This book exists thanks to their dedicated preservation of the past:

Michael Del Castello
Dan Driskell
Bob Fulwider
Eldon Garrett
Larry Johnson
Tom Lennon

Robert Martin
Dave Palmer
Terry Persons
Tom Pfeiffer
David Rubinson
Jim Smock

And special thanks to:
Bill and Lillian Butterfield

We would like to thank the following people for their assistance and cooperation in the preparation of this book:

Frank Adams
Russell Allard
Rick Botts
John Cornelius
Steve Cottrell

John Garlow
Jean Greendyke
Steve Loots
Dawn Patrick
Dick Schuettge

INDEX